Looking at Transport

Looking at
Cars

Cliff Lines

Looking at Transport

Looking at Cars
Looking at Submarines
Looking at Buses
Looking at Trucks
Looking at Merchant Ships
Looking at Motor Bikes
Looking at Passenger Aircraft
Looking at Trains

*This book is based on an
original text by Cyril Posthumus*

First published in 1984 by
Wayland (Publishers) Ltd
49 Lansdowne Place, Hove
East Sussex BN3 1HF, England

© Copyright 1984 Wayland (Publishers) Ltd

ISBN 0 85078 429 8

Phototypeset by Kalligraphics Ltd, Redhill, Surrey
Printed in Italy by G. Canale & C.S.p.A., Turin
Bound in the UK by The Pitman Press, Bath

Contents

Carriages without horses

Today many families have a motor car.
They are part of everyday life and are very useful.
Most cars carry up to five people and their luggage.
They are fairly comfortable and take people from place
to place quickly.
Cars run on petrol and oil and need a check up
from time to time.
Fifty years ago very few people owned cars.

Before cars, road journeys were made by coach.
Coaches were expensive and uncomfortable.
The fare was lower if you sat outside with the driver.

This is one of the first railway trains.
This strange sight made people stop and stare.
The engine was driven by steam.
The second coach is like the one on page 4.
Nearly all the passengers sat in the open.

One hundred years ago there were no cars.
Horses were used instead and the roads were
dotted with heaps of manure.
Roads were bumpy as there was no hard top to them.
In summer they were dusty and in winter they were
covered in mud.

This strange machine was made over 200 years ago.
It was built to pull a heavy gun along the road.
It was the first road machine with its own power.
Steam power was used to move it slowly along.
Every few minutes it ran dry and more water was added.

Many coaches using steam power were built in Britain
about 150 years ago.
They were very heavy and slow and they often broke down.
In 1865 a law was passed to limit the speed of road vehicles.
They could not go faster than 6.5 km per hour (4 m.p.h.).
Someone had to walk in front carrying a red flag
during the day and a red lamp after dark.
This law stopped inventors in Britain from trying to
build better and faster machines.
Instead, other countries like Germany tried out new ideas.

This coach was driven by a steam engine.
There were chimneys at the back to get rid of the smoke.
The driver steered it by turning the two front wheels.
There were no rubber tyres and the roads were poor so
the passengers had a bumpy journey.
Once the railways were built these carriages were
no longer used.

Steam engines needed water for the boiler.
They also had to carry loads of coal to
keep the fire burning.
Two men were needed to keep the engine going.
One was the driver and the other stoked the fire.
The engines could not go far before more water and
coal were needed.
Steam was not the best kind of power and
other kinds were looked for.

The inventor of this carriage used a large container
of coal gas to drive the engine.
It was not very powerful and was big and heavy.
Not enough gas could be carried to drive it very far.

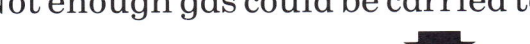

Some inventors tried to use electricity to drive cars.
The electricity had to be stored in heavy batteries
underneath the car.

Oil from under the ground had been used for a long
time to make lamp oil, wax and other oils.
In Germany inventors began to build engines that
used petrol, which was also made from oil.
An engineer called Gottlieb Daimler had the idea of
mixing the gas from petrol with air and making it explode.
The force of the explosion would drive the engine.

This coach was built by Daimler.
It was one of the first to have a petrol-driven engine.
It was really a horse-drawn coach with the shafts
and the horse taken away.
There was only one passenger seat because
the other was needed for the engine.
The man in the passenger seat is Daimler himself.

At the same time as Daimler was building his first
horseless carriage, Karl Benz was also
making a petrol engine.
The two men lived in towns only 96 kilometres
(60 miles) apart.
Neither inventor knew that the other was
working on the same idea.
Everything was kept secret because the inventors
were afraid of having their ideas stolen.
Daimler told his workmen that his coach must be a
secret because it was a present for his wife.

Before he started working on petrol engines
Karl Benz made gas engines like this one.
They were used to drive machinery, not cars.

Benz built a petrol engine to power a motor car.
He also invented the sparking plug.
This was connected to a battery and made a spark
which exploded the gas inside the engine.

This is a three-wheeled Benz car of 100 years ago.
The engine drove the back wheels by using a belt and chains.
The driver and passenger could sit side by side.

New ideas in France and Germany

This is the first motor car to be advertised and put on sale to the public.
It was made by Benz and was called the 'Patent Motorcarriage'.
It could travel at 16 kilometres per hour (10 m.p.h.).

There were many problems to solve before people wanted to buy cars.
They were a novelty and very expensive.

In 1891 Benz built this car with four wheels.
It was called the 'Viktoria'.
It still looked like a horse-drawn carriage.
A fold-back roof made it possible for the driver and
passengers to stay dry when it rained.

Benz's next car was called the 'Velo'.
It was lighter and cheaper than the 'Viktoria'
and could travel at 20 km/h (12½ m.p.h.).
By 1895 Benz had sold more than 100 'Velos'.

This is a drawing of an early Daimler motor carriage.
The petrol engine is at the front.
Passengers sat facing one another behind the driver.

Daimler was also making petrol cars.
One of them was called the *Stahlrad* or
'steel-wheeler' because its wheels had
wire spokes instead of wooden ones.
Daimler's *Stahlrad* was shown at a display in Paris in 1889.
One of the people who was interested in it
was called Armand Peugeot.
He was the owner of a firm making tools and
other metal goods.
He liked the car so much he decided to make cars
at his own factory.

In 1890 the first Peugeot car was made and
it was a great success.
Today, Peugeot is one of the largest car-making firms
in France.

Another car made in France at this time was
the Panhard-Levassor.
It was named after the two Frenchmen who built it,
Réné Panhard and Emile Levassor.

Early cars were steered by a lever called the 'cow's tail'.

In 1891 Panhard built a car with the engine at the front.
This was a better place for the engine because
it could be cooled by the air as the car moved.
Panhard's car was the first to have its engine at the front,
but most cars now have the engine there.

One Panhard car was driven for 41 years
without any major troubles.
It covered 241,000 kilometres (150,000 miles).

The first car rally was held in France in 1894.
More than 100 cars entered but only 21 actually started.
Thirteen of them were petrol driven and
the others used steam.
All thirteen petrol cars finished the distance of
127 kilometres (79 miles).
The prize for the most practical car was shared by
Panhard and Peugeot.
Both of these cars had Daimler engines.

Here is a petrol car of the 1890s.
By that time cars were beginning to look much more solid as
more parts were made of metal instead of wood.

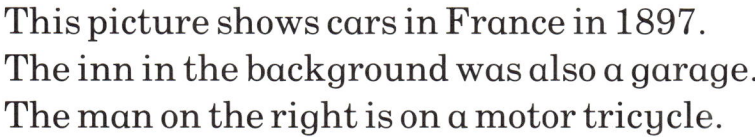

This picture shows cars in France in 1897.
The inn in the background was also a garage.
The man on the right is on a motor tricycle.

Here is one of the first motor car races.

The first real car race was held in France in 1895.
A distance of more than 1,100 km (700 miles)
had to be covered in three days.
The fastest car in the race was driven by Emile Levassor.
He drove for over 48 hours with only one short stop.
His average speed was 24 km/h (15 m.p.h.).

This is John Dunlop who invented the first
air-filled rubber tyre.
He first used air-filled rubber tyres for
cycle racing.

Two brothers, called Michelin, fitted air-filled tyres
to a Peugeot car for the 1895 car race.
During the race the car had many punctures, but in
a few years all cars had 'pneumatic' tyres.
The Michelin and Dunlop companies are both famous today
for their tyres.

All of these changes were taking place outside Britain.
This was because it was against the law to
drive at more than 6.5 km/h (4 m.p.h.) in Britain and
a man had to walk in front of a car waving a red flag.
These laws were changed in 1896 and a special car run
was held from London to Brighton to celebrate.
Every year in November the same run is held.
It is called the London to Brighton Veteran Run.
Only very old cars, called 'veterans', take part.

Cars for the rich

By the year 1900 cars were no longer stared at in wonder.
Many more countries were starting to make cars but
only rich people could afford to buy them.

This is a French de Dion car.
The wheels had pneumatic tyres but
steering was still done by a lever.

A tyre pump, head lamp, hats with ear protectors, and
a horn which motorists could buy eighty years ago.
The lamp burned gas and the horn was worked by
squeezing the rubber bulb.

At the beginning of the twentieth century
France was still the leading country for making cars.
A firm called de Dion made a cheap, light engine which
could be fitted into cars and other road vehicles.
Other firms began making car parts such as
frames and gearboxes.
Some makers bought these parts, put them into cars,
and sold them under their own name.

A young Frenchman called Louis Renault took a de Dion
engine and put it into a frame to make a small car.
It went so well he made several more for his friends.
Soon he moved into a factory and made many more cars.
His small car won races and became very popular.
The de Dion firm also started making cars.
By 1904 they were the largest car firm in the world.

In Germany Daimler's son Paul built a new car
with many improvements on the old Canstatt-Daimlers.
He was persuaded to do this by a man called Emil Jellinek.
Jellinek promised to buy 36 of Daimler's new cars,
provided the name was changed to Mercedes.
Mercedes was his daughter's name.
This is the first Mercedes motor car.
It was really the first sports car.

This British racing car was made by a firm called Napier.
It won first prize in a race in 1902.

British car firms were becoming well known too.
Early makes were Wolseley, Napier and Rolls-Royce.
A Wolseley won a long distance race in 1900 and
Napier cars also won several important races.
In 1905 a Napier broke the world land speed record
at 168 km/h (104 m.p.h.).

Here is a racing car in 1905.
The engine is very long and large and
it is cooled by a radiator filled with water.
The wheels are smaller than in earlier cars.

Rolls-Royce are the most famous British cars.
They took their name from Henry Royce and Charles Rolls.
Royce was a skilful engineer and Rolls was a rich sportsman.
It was Rolls who made the Rolls-Royce into a luxury car.
It has remained famous for its high quality ever since.

Inventors in the United States of America were
very interested in the cars being made in Europe.
Some cars had been built in the USA but
they were not very successful.
Then the Duryea brothers made a reliable car and
started the first American car factory.

This is a Duryea car of about 1898.

Here is an American Oldsmobile car with a rounded front.
It was called a 'Curved Dash' because of its shape.
It was steered by a 'cow's tail' and
the engine was at the back under the floor.

Many firms in the United States started to make cars.
When James Packard complained about a car he had
bought the makers told him to see if he could do better.
He did, and his Packard cars became famous.
One of the best known and most expensive cars in America
is the Cadillac.
The first one was made in 1903.
Parts for each Cadillac were exactly alike.
Three Cadillacs were taken apart and the parts were
mixed up and then put back together again.
All three cars worked perfectly on a test run.

Early cars were made one by one by groups of workers.
The Americans invented a way of making cars
quickly and cheaply.
Parts were added as a line of cars moved around the factory.
Each worker did the same job on each car as it passed.
Henry Ford became famous for making cars in this way.
His factory made only one type of car — the Model T.
It was easy to drive, strong and cheap.

This is part of Henry Ford's car factory.
As the partly made cars moved along,
more parts were added by workers.

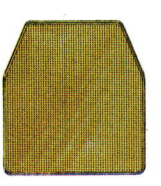

P D - Wagen, 1900

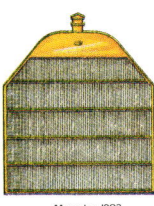

Mercedes, 1903

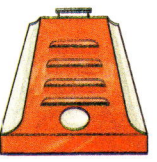

Opel Darracq, 1903

Rolls Royce, 1904

Designers tried to make the cars look attractive.
They also wanted people to know who the maker was.
So they used special shapes for such parts as the radiators.

Workers in the Ford factory did the same job all day but they were well paid and people wanted to work there.
The model T was cheap enough for many people to be able to buy one.
Because it was cheap people made jokes about it.
One was: 'What's the time when two Fords pass one another? Tin past tin'.

Cars for everyone

The more cars that were made, the cheaper they became.
America became the country making the most cars.
The United States is very large and cars have become
the most important way of getting around.
A large company called General Motors started in 1908.
Over the years General Motors has bought many other
car firms in America and Europe.
It now owns firms such as Vauxhall, Cadillac, Chevrolet
and Opel.

This picture shows cars on an
American road fifty years ago.
There were fewer cars on the roads
then than there are today.

By fifty years ago cars had become similar to
one another in many ways.
They all had three pedals, a gear lever and a handbrake.
But some people wanted cars that looked smart.
If they had enough money they could buy a car like
the one in the picture.

In 1938 a car with the engine at the back appeared.
It was the Volkswagen (VW) or 'People's Car' and
it was nicknamed 'the Beetle' because of its shape.

During the Second World War (1939–45) the only cars made
were for use by the army.
At the end of the war many people wanted to buy cars.
In Britain factories changed from making tanks to
making cars like the Morris Minor and the Jaguar.
In Germany new factories were built and
thousands of Beetles were made.

Over 20 million Beetles were made up to 1978.
Today other VW cars have taken the Beetle's place but
you can still see Beetles on the road.
Many other firms started making cheap cars.
In America cars looked different — big and ugly
with huge bumpers and tail fins.
Many Americans could afford large cars and
petrol was cheap in their country.

In 1960 a new small car went on sale in Britain.
It was called the Mini and it became very popular.
Here is the man who designed the Mini standing beside
the first one that was made.
On the left of the picture is the first Morris Minor.

Roads had to be made better for the thousands of cars which used them.
Motorways were designed without crossroads so that traffic could travel fast over long distances.
Motorways were first built in Italy and Germany.
In America similar roads were built between the main cities.
The first important motorway in Britain was the M1.
Many countries in the world now have motorways.

This is a view of a freeway in California, USA.
It is called a freeway because you do not have to pay to use it.
On some roads in America and elsewhere you must pay a toll.
California has some of the best roads in the world.
They are needed because nearly everyone has a car.

Not all cars were as safe as they should have been.
The American firm of General Motors made a car
called the Corvair which was dangerous to drive.
A man named Ralph Nader wrote a book to warn people
about the Corvair and other cars that were unsafe.
As a result strict safety laws were made which
car makers had to obey.

This is Ralph Nader.

This picture shows a layer of 'smog' hanging over Athens in Greece.

Smog is caused by car exhaust fumes.
It is poisonous and can make people ill.
In 1970 the government in the USA passed the Clean Air Act.
Car-makers had to build cars that produced less dangerous exhaust fumes.

This is a modern Japanese car, the Mazda RX7.
The headlamps are hidden under hoods which lift when
a button inside the car is pushed.

Twenty-five years ago Japan made very few cars.
They began building new car factories and
making new cars that sold overseas.
People found that Japanese cars were well built and
cheaper than other cars.
Today Japan makes more cars than any other country.
Japanese cars are sold all over the world and
as a result other firms sell fewer cars.

How a car works

The three most important parts of a car are the wheels,
the body and the engine.
Two of the wheels are turned by the engine.
In some cars the front wheels are driven but
in others it is the back wheels.
The driver uses the steering wheel to steer the car.
A pedal called the accelerator is pushed down
to make the car go faster.
There is a brake pedal to make the car stop.

Many different parts are needed to make the engine.
Workers add parts as the engines move past on a belt.

There are many moving parts inside the engine.
They help to turn the crankshaft and
the crankshaft turns two of the car's wheels.
Oil keeps the parts moving smoothly.

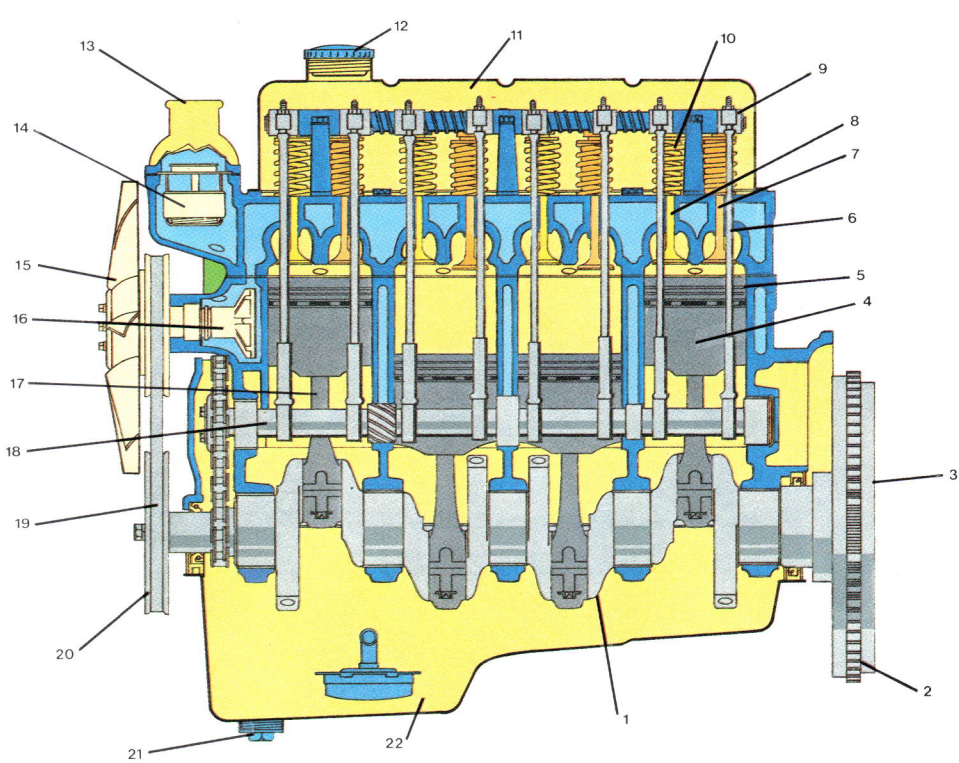

Looking at an engine

1 Crankshaft
2 Starter ring
3 Flywheel
4 Piston
5 Piston rings
6 Push rod
7 Outlet valve
8 Inlet valve
9 Rocker shaft
10 Valve spring
11 Rocker box cover

12 Engine oil cap
13 Radiator cap
14 Thermostat
15 Fan
16 Water pump
17 Piston connecting rod
18 Camshaft
19 Fan belt
20 Fan pulley
21 Oil drain plug
22 Sump

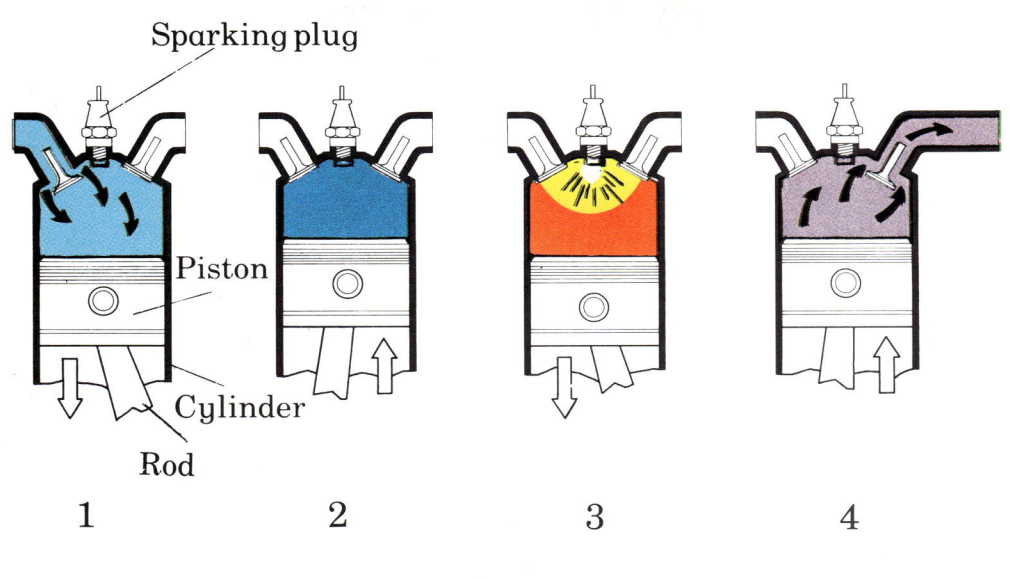

Sparking plug

Piston

Cylinder

Rod

1   2   3   4

This part of the engine is called the cylinder.
Cars usually have four or six cylinders.
Inside the cylinder there is a piston joined by a rod
to the crankshaft.
At the top of the cylinder there is a sparking plug
which is wired to an electric battery.
Gas from petrol is mixed with air and then
this mixture is sucked into the cylinder.
A spark from the sparking plug makes the gas explode.
The force of the explosion pushes down the piston.
When the piston moves down the crankshaft is turned.

The four pictures above show what happens in the cylinder.
1. A mixture of air and gas is sucked into the
   cylinder as the piston moves down.
2. The piston moves up squeezing the air and gas.
3. A spark from the sparking plug makes the gas explode
   and the piston is pushed down.
4. The piston moves up, pushing out all the burnt gas.

The body of the car is sprayed
many times with paint.
Paint stops the car from going rusty.
The men wear masks to protect them
from the paint.

The driver starts the car by turning a key.
This switches on the electricity and the engine starts.
When the engine is running it becomes very hot.
To keep it cool it is surrounded by a metal jacket
filled with water.
The water comes from the radiator where it is kept cool
by air and a fan.
It is pumped round the engine by an electric pump.
The power of the engine is taken to the wheels
through a clutch and a gearbox.
Many cars have a clutch pedal.
When the driver pushes the pedal down, power from
the engine is stopped from reaching the wheels and
the driver can then move the gear lever.
When the driver changes the position of the gear lever
the speed of the engine changes.
When the car is in a low gear it goes slowly.
In a high gear it goes fast.
The gear lever is also used to make the car go backwards.

Some cars do not have a clutch pedal.
Instead they have a lever which can be moved to the
letters P (parking), R (reverse), N (neutral) and D (drive).
To go forwards the lever is moved to D and
as the car goes faster it changes gear automatically.
P and N are used when the car is not moving and
R is used to make the car go backwards.

Electricity from the battery goes to the engine,
the lights and the instruments in front of the driver.
Power goes along a shaft to the back wheels.
This shaft is part of the 'transmission'.
Springs near the wheels give the car a smooth ride.
The springs are part of the car's 'suspension'.

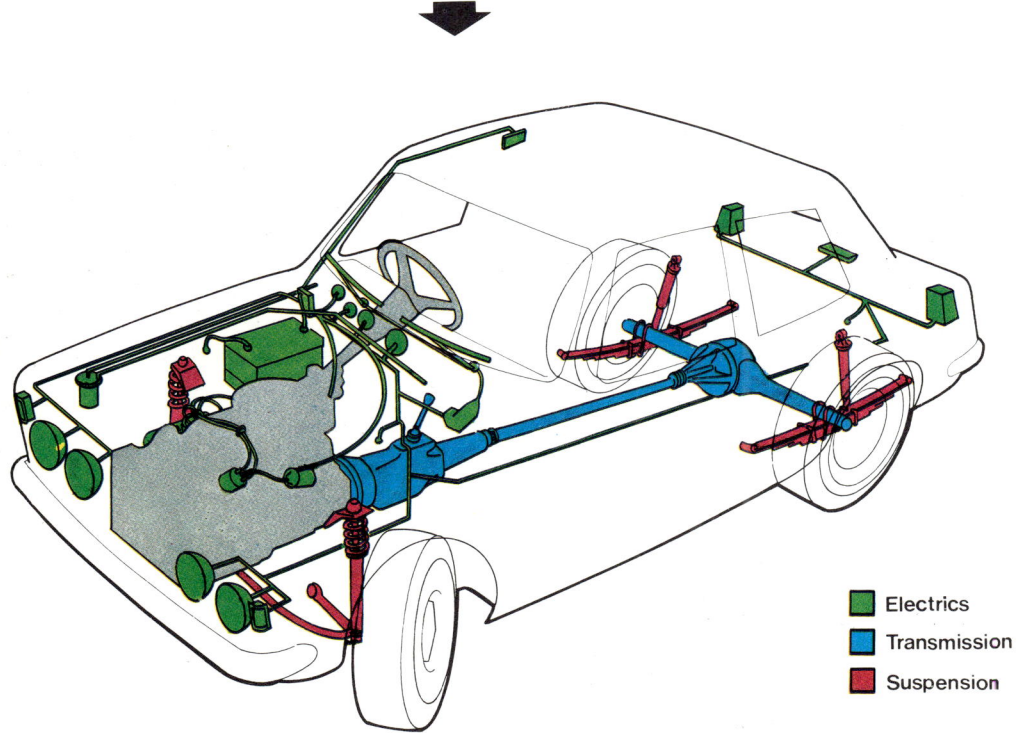

■ Electrics
■ Transmission
■ Suspension

The Mini car was first made in Britain in 1960.
To make the car very small the engine was placed
sideways and it drove the front wheels.
There is more space inside the car because
a shaft to the back wheels is not needed.
The Mini is a light car but it is very strong.
It is very popular and other car makers
have copied some of the ideas used in it.

Notice how small the Mini's wheels are and
how near to the ground the body is.

This car worker is checking a new Ford which
has just been made.
He must note down faults so that they can be
put right before the car leaves the factory.

Steering large, heavy cars can be hard work.
In some cars steering is made easier by using power to help
turn the wheels.
Power is also used to make the brakes easier to use.
There is a brake on each wheel of the car.
The brake pedal works all the brakes but the hand brake
only works those on the back wheels.

Living with cars

Cars have changed our way of life.
Thanks to cars people do not need to
live close to where they work.
They can travel to work by car.
Houses are built with garages, and the places we visit,
such as shopping centres, need large car parks.

This is a drive-in bank in America.
Customers drive up to a window and do their business
without getting out of their cars.

![Drive-in bank photograph]

Cars can drive straight on to this hovercraft which
takes them across the English Channel to France.

Villages and towns some way from cities have become
popular places for people to live.
It is possible to drive to work in a city and
live in the countryside.
Cars also allow people in towns and cities to drive
to the countryside and the coast in their spare time.

In towns and cities car parking is a problem.
Large multi-storey car parks have been built.

Roads sometimes need to be built through large cities.
This can be very expensive as buildings must be
knocked down and land bought at high prices.

Traffic has also brought other problems.
People who live near busy roads complain about the noise.
Motorways and garages can spoil the beauty and
peace of the countryside.
These problems can be reduced by planning carefully.

As more and more people use cars the number of
accidents has increased.
Laws have been passed to make driving safer.
All drivers must pass a driving test.
In Britain, seat belts must be worn by people in
the front seats.
Some other countries have the same law and
it has helped to save many lives.

Car firms have also started to design safer cars.
The car frame is made strong enough to protect people
inside even if the car is hit or rolls over.
Special brakes have been designed to stop cars from
skidding and tyres have been made safer.

This car is being made by robots.
The sparks are made when the robot machines weld
(join together) metal parts.
One man at a control panel can check the work done
by a team of robots.

Many thousands of people work in the car industry.
As well as the workers in the car factories
there are many others making parts and
selling or repairing cars.
The number of car workers is going down now.
This is because many of the unpleasant jobs are
being done by machines.

These cars are moving along a production line
in a car factory.
The workers have to attach new parts as
the cars move past them.
They must work at a steady speed to keep up with the cars.

Cars are made in many countries of the world.
The countries which make the most cars are
Japan, the USA, West Germany and France.

Large car firms now have factories in several countries.
Some Vauxhall cars sold in Britain are made in Spain.
Parts made in other countries are put into cars made in Britain,
and parts made in Britain are sent to
car factories in other countries.

There are now so many cars on the road that
traffic jams are a big problem in cities.
This picture was taken during the
afternoon rush hour in a French city.

Ideas for the future

This ship is exploring for oil
under the sea-bed.
There is a round helicopter pad on
the ship and a small supply boat
alongside.
The tower holds a steel drill.
Large oil wells have been found
under the sea.

One day the petrol needed to drive cars will be used up.
Scientists are looking for other kinds of power to
take the place of petrol.
Electricity is used to drive milk delivery vans but
they cannot travel far or very fast.
Electric power needs large and heavy batteries which
soon run down and must be changed or charged up.
The advantages of electricity are that it is clean and quiet.

This car is driven by electric batteries.
It is small and light and ideal for short trips.
One day it is hoped someone will invent a battery
that will store a lot of electricity for a long time.

Another idea is to put an electric cable under roads.
The power could be picked up by cars as they
travelled over the cable.
One answer to the power problem may be to have cars
which make their own electricity.
A petrol engine would drive an electric motor and
this would power the car.
It will not work properly until large amounts of
electricity can be stored in light, small containers.
Some petrol would still be needed,
but less than for a normal car.

This unusual looking car uses power from the sun.
The car may look strange but so did the first
horseless carriages.

A new kind of engine has been fitted into
a Japanese Mazda car.
It is called the Wankel engine after its German inventor.
A Mazda car fitted with this engine won a race at
Silverstone, England, in 1981.
There are fewer dangerous gases from this engine.
It is small, smooth running and light but
it uses more petrol than other engines.

Another new engine is the gas turbine.
Some aircraft and ships have gas-turbine engines.
One was tried in a car but it burned too much fuel.
Gas turbines are also very expensive to make.
Here is a cut-away view of a gas-turbine engine.
It has many more parts than a petrol engine.

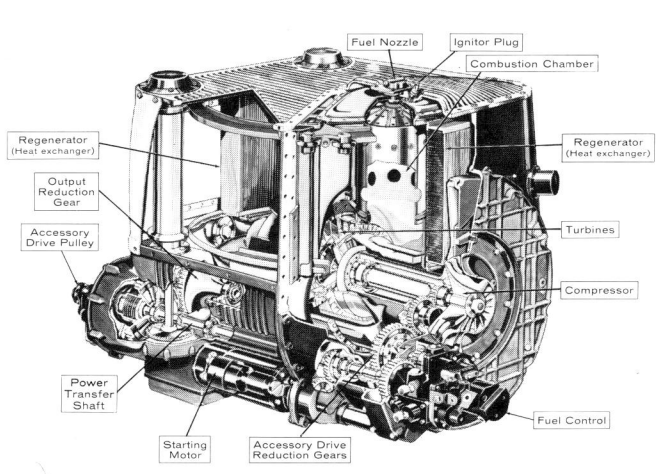

Gas from the oil and gas fields under the sea may
be the fuel for engines of the future.
The gas is turned into a liquid and used in a car engine.
It does not give off dangerous gases so it is clean.
Unfortunately the special engine needed is expensive.
The liquid gas must also be stored in large and
heavy containers.

Many racing cars have turbo-superchargers.
A supercharger gives the car extra power by
using the exhaust gases from the engine.
This burns up the dangerous gases and
leaves the air clean.

This is sugar cane growing in South America.
In Brazil a kind of alcohol is made from the cane.
This alcohol is mixed into petrol and used to power cars.
This means that less petrol is used.

Lorries, taxis and some cars have diesel engines.
Diesel oil goes further than petrol, and costs less.

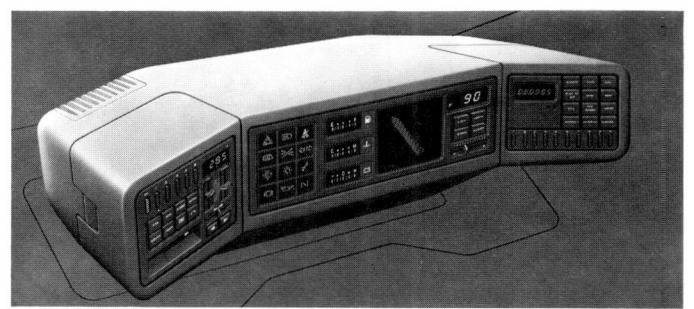

This is what a car's dashboard may look like one day.
Rows of figures and lights will be worked by
a computer linked to different parts of the car.

Some expensive cars already have computers to
give the driver information.
By pushing buttons the driver can find out many things
about the car — how much petrol he is using,
what is left in the tank, or what the temperature is
outside the car.
Computers may one day make it possible for the driver
to feed in information about where he wants to go and
the computer will then drive the car for him.
New inventions will make driving easier and safer
in the future.

Glossary

Battery   A container that stores electricity.

Coal gas   Gas which is produced when coal is heated.

Crankshaft   The rod inside the engine which is turned by the up-and-down movement of the pistons.

Cylinder   The part of the engine in which the mixture of gas and air is exploded.
A piston moves up and down inside the cylinder.

Gas-turbine engine   An engine in which a rotor (fan) is turned by burning gases, and the turning rotor drives the wheels of the car.

Gearbox   A box near the engine which allows the driver to change the speed of the car by moving the gear lever.

Multi-storey   A building with several floors.

Pneumatic tyre   A tyre that is filled with air.

Production line   A way of making cars: partly made cars move along on a conveyor and car workers add more parts as the cars pass them.

Radiator   The part of a car which holds the water that is used to cool the engine.

Smog   The word comes from SMoke and fOG.
Smog is a grey cloud of harmful gases that forms in some cities, due to car exhaust fumes.

Sparking plug   The part of a car that makes the spark which explodes the gas inside the cylinder.

Suspension   The springs and shock absorbers in a car that help to give the passengers a smooth ride.

Veteran car   A car made before 1919, and especially one made before 1905.

Index

Picture acknowledgements

The illustrations in this book were supplied by: Britax 51; British Leyland 35, 46, 52; British Transport Films 49; J. Allen Cash 60 (top); Dunlop Ltd. 21; Electricity Council 56; Ford Motor Co. 30, 31 (bottom), 41, 44, 47, 53; General Motors Corporation 29; John Laing and Sons Ltd. 50; Mazda Car Imports (GB) Ltd. 40; Mercedes-Benz *front cover*, 11, 12, 13, 14; Topham 19, 20, 27, 32, 33, 37, 38, 39, 48, 54, 57, 60 (bottom); V.A.G. (United Kingdom) Ltd. 34.